In Awesome Praise...

Jill MorGan

This book is dedicated to Carole and Glenda, faithful and encouraging friends, with whom it is such an honour and privilege to be walking together in serving the Lord.

'Your words became a joy and the delight of my heart.'
Jeremiah 15:16

<u>RESTORATION</u>

Psalm 145, Mark 16:17-20, 1 John 5:14,
Revelation 4:11

God, I am in wonder of Your constant love. Daily I
praise You because You are worthy to be
worshipped.
All the glory and honour of the nations are due to
You. May Your name be magnified, and the
greatness of Your power be made known in every
land as supernatural healings break out.
Let every broken and diseased body be renewed
and made whole by Your word and the might of
Your hand.
Let signs and wonders accompany Your people
and be made manifest in these times. Lord,
whatever You need to do to make us ready to
work out Your will and purposes. Do within us
that Your Kingdom might be seen and come upon
the earth.
Amen.

UNCHANGEABLE

Psalm 136, Psalm 138, Lamentations 3:22-23

Faithful God, You are so unchanging.
Every morning that I wake, Your mercy is there to
cover me, and Your cup of eternal love is prepared
to fill me afresh.
You dwell in the heights of the heavens and make
Yourself known in the artistry of the skies. Your
powerful fire of glory is revealed through the
brightness of the sun and reflected by the light of
the moon amongst the darkness.
You have made Yourself known in every detail of
creation, speaking openly of Your death and
resurrection life through the life cycles of trees,
flowers, and plants.
Every bird sings of Your glory, every animal plays
its own part in Your plans.
We were made for Your glory and purpose
therefore reveal Yourself, through us O Lord.
Amen.

TONGUE OF THE TRINITY

*Exodus 14:21, 1 Kings 8:10 –11, Isaiah 41:10,
Matthew 16:16, John 17:17, Romans 11:33*

The awesomeness of who You are as God is
hidden in Your mystery as Father, Son and Holy
Spirit.
The mystery of this threefold identity and the
ways You share as one God are too hard for man
to understand; for to see You as You are, is to gaze
into the brightness of Your glory.
Your presence is too powerful for any man to
stand before You and look upon You without
falling to the ground.
The strength of Your righteous right hand parted
the sea whilst the wind of Your Spirit moved the
unmoveable.
Who cannot hear Your voice thunder and not pay
attention to the pure truth within Your words?
Your blood cleanses bringing new birth and
eternal life.
Everything moves at Your command for You are
the living God, yesterday, today, and forever.
Amen.

GUIDED INTO PURPOSE

Deuteronomy 31:8, 2 Chronicles 16:9,
Psalm 119, Isaiah 45:2 −7

You are my guide, O Great Jehovah.
Your constant presence goes before me, making
every path straight and assuring me that I will
never be left to face things on my own.
Daily I hear You calling me by my name,
revealing Your plans and Your hand upon me.
You are my Lord and there is no other. No-one
else can show me the goodness and mercy You
give throughout every day of my life.
When You speak to me, the way before me is
revealed and I can boldly advance knowing
nothing can separate me from Your love.
Your heart longs for someone to share Your life
with. Daily You search for someone who will give
themselves wholly to You in obedience and
embrace You as their source of strength.
Lord strengthen me that I might walk with You.
Amen.

KINGDOM THINKING

Exodus 3:14, Isaiah 55:8,
Matthew 6:33, Matthew 19:26, James 5:16

Lord God Almighty, Your thoughts and ways are
far higher than those known on the earth. As the
great "I Am" it is impossible for You to think or
act as man does.
Your Spirit is holy and therefore can only operate
according to the life and decrees of Your
Kingdom.
How You must long for us to think and move
according to the ways of the Spirit and come into
alignment with You by sitting at Your feet.
Train us in Your righteousness that our prayers
might both reflect Your will and strengthen our
faith that with You, all things are possible.
Lord You know the desires of our hearts therefore
lead us to seek first the Kingdom of God that we
might bring blessing and the glory to Your name.
Amen.

FORGIVING FATHER

Psalm 23, John 14, John 14:6

Father God, Your love and faithfulness
endures forever. Your promises never fail.
Every word You give is true and leads us deeper
into Your ways of life.
You are the great Shepherd of the sheep whose
rod and staff brings us into alignment and deeper
relationship with You.
Father, You are always ready and willing to
encounter us in our need and to hear and respond
to our heartfelt cries.
Teach us, as Your children, to love and honour
Your commands and strengthen our trust in Your
words for it is through them that You reveal the
fullness of all that You are.
Amen.

OVERCOMING LOVE

Genesis 2:7, Luke 13:34, Luke 15:10
John 16:33, Hebrews 12:2-3

Lord, Your holiness is beyond comprehension.
Before it the angels bow down in adoration and
offer You their praise.
Much greater their celebration must be when
Your glory is revealed, as one repentant man
turns from their unbelief.
How You must long to gather into Your arms
those who are lost and without purpose, that they
might know the greatness of Your victorious love
amidst the troubles of this world.
Help us to fix our eyes upon You, pursue an
understanding of Your heart and walk in all Your
ways.
You are the Great Giver of Life, the
very air we breathe comes from You alone.
Amen.

WISDOM AT WORK

Daniel 2:20-23, Psalm 111:9

Holy and awesome is Your name, O Lord. Every
act of Your hand is honourable and glorious.
Your wonderful works will be remembered from
age to age, generation after generation will speak
of Your holy Word.
You are always gracious and compassionate
towards us, and Your promises never fail.
Wisdom is imparted within our hearts as we
honour You. Praise and worship
brings things to birth within our lives.
Your wisdom, O God is the source of changing
times and seasons. By Your words governing,
authorities are either raised up or removed.
Those who understand Your heart grow wise.
With understanding they navigate the times for
You reveal the deep and secret things to them.
You know all that lies ahead. You perceive what is
unknown in the darkness because light dwells in
You.
Amen.

MOVEMENT ABOUNDS

Psalm 139, John 3:8, 1 Corinthians 1:25

Lord You created the universe, giving each star an identity and telling the planets where they should dwell.
You climbed into Your chariot and the wings of the seraphim led You to view the rising dawn that would bring life to all the inhabitants of the earth.
The wind of the Spirit blew across the earth, invisible to the mortal eye and unrestrained by human hand.
Even now the presence of Your Holy Spirit moves across the nations bringing divine wisdom from the Godhead: Father, Son and Holy Spirit.
By bringing man into obedience to Your will, You reveal that Your ways are wiser than human wisdom, and that a broken and contrite heart is stronger than any human strength.
Praise be to You, Lord.
Amen.

TEACHING AND TRANSFORMATION

Hebrews 9:14

Father God, You sent Your Spirit to give us both
eternal life in the Heavens and abundant life
whilst on the earth.
Your Spirit teaches us by witnessing to what You
have spoken and revealing Your great desire for
relationship with us.
Every command You have given in Your Word
becomes a testimony of Your power and greatness
in our lives.
Father, as we wait upon You, overwhelm us by
breaking into our lives with Your glorious
presence. Transform lives and birth within our
hearts a new heavenly language that magnifies
Your name.
Lord, increase our capacity that Your life might
fully dwell within us and burst forth from us
as a witness to the truth of Your word today.
Amen.

PERFECT SACRIFICE

1 Peter 1:19

I will declare Your holiness and Your mighty
power, O God, the beauty of Your glory.
Even now Your eyes are searching for those whose
hearts are pure, whose lives are set apart for You,
that You might send Your fire upon them.
By the power of Your Holy Spirit, I ask You to
remove every displeasing and unclean thing in my
life that I might draw closer to You and never be
separated from Your love.
Open my ears to Your voice every day and impart
into my heart the desire and discipline
to walk in obedience to Your will.
Amen.

HELD IN WONDER

Psalm 24:1-2

Lord God, You hold the world within Your hands.
You alone are the King of life, and Your glory is
witnessed throughout the earth.
Through the sacrifice of Your Son, Jesus, His life
became ours and when He was raised through the
power of the Holy Spirit our lives were raised also.
Who then can deny Your glory or escape the fear
of the Lord?
It is in embracing these that we begin to walk on
Your paths of wisdom
You alone are the great "I AM" and everything
that is remains under Your feet.
As the world grows darker, may the light of Your
life shine and grow brighter within Your people,
to the glory of Your name.
Amen.

IMAGE OF THE INVISIBLE

1 Timothy 1:17

Great and Holy God, You are the true Father of all mankind.
Although invisible to our eyes, in Your great mercy You chose to reveal Your image through Your Son, Jesus, and in doing so showed us a perfect image of ourselves.
How amazing are the works of Your hands, for having designed the blueprint for our image and lives, You carefully hand crafted us within our mother's womb.
Truly we are fearfully and wonderfully made for Your purposes. Your word leads us on the path of life and Your power in us reveals Your glory.
It is in the refining of our hearts by Your words of fire that our eyes are opened to see You as You truly are, and it is by the baptism of Your Holy Spirit that we can enter our true position within Your Kingdom.
There we will worship, praise, and serve You eternally as our King of kings.
Amen.

FAITHFUL TO FORGIVE

2 Corinthians 1:20

Lord, when You give us a promise, You are
faithful to keep it and prove it to be true.
It is impossible for any word You speak over us to
come to nothing for in Your favour and mercy You
ensure that it will come to pass.
Even when it seems too late, You come with the
invitation to receive Your forgiveness and return
to the life and purpose You first spoke over us.
No one can be hidden from Your eyes for You
relentlessly pursue us to show us and lead us into
Your life.
It is because of Your great love that the prodigals
return home, the hungry are fed, the thirsty
receive water and the broken heart is mended.
You ensure that presence is ever before us by
constantly drawing our gaze back to You; for You
will allow nothing to separate us from Your love.
Every day You walk with us, for in Your love You
cannot bear to leave us or turn away from us.
Amen.

GREAT I AM

Exodus 3:14

Father, when You spoke to Moses, You revealed Your name to be "I AM".
The fullness of life that that name held was revealed in the very beginning when, as both Father and Creator, You called all things into being through the voice of Your Son, and breathed life into them through the Holy Spirit. It was at Your call they moved, at Your spoken word they came into being, and at Your command they were brought back into life and purpose.
You are the great restorer. Daily, You put Your plans into action, often through invisible processes, knowing that these will bring glory to Your name.
You loved the world so much that You revealed Yourself in human form through Your son, making the life and power within Your name available to all who would believe. As His blood was poured out at the cross so Your life was poured out, not for a one-time restoration from sin, but to give us life eternally.
Make me clean, Lord. Amen.

INSPIRED TO SPEAK

Psalm 9:9, Matthew 11:5

Lord God, You are lifted high above all people.
Daily they praise Your great and awesome name
and recognise Your holiness.
Every Scripture that we read was inspired by You,
O God. Through Your prophets, priests and
chosen ones, You declared Your Word and in
doing so You revealed Yourself.
Across the nations there are many who can
witness to seeing and experiencing Your mighty
works and wonders. Even today, the blind see, the
deaf hear, the lame walk and the dead are raised
by the power of Your words.
Whenever the poor have the Gospel preached to
them, You reveal Yourself anew. Every word
spoken testifies to the truth that Your Son, Jesus
Christ was and still is the promised Messiah:
deliverer, healer and saviour to the glory to Your
name.
Amen.

CREATION CALLS

Psalm 8, Psalm 104

Lord the excellence of Your name is declared
throughout all the earth.
By Your words the foundations of the earth were
laid and set. According to Your blueprints the
boundaries for the sea were drawn and set.
Your love and mercy cover the tiniest detail, for
You readily give food both to the birds of the air
and the fish in the sea.
Whenever You open Your hand and reveal Your
power, we are blessed. When we walk among the
trees and look at the beauty of each plant, they
openly speak of Your strength and splendour.
Everywhere we look, You reveal Yourself to be
the awesome artist whether in the colours of the
earth or the masterpieces drawn within the sky.
Each cloud moves silently above the earth,
alternatively being lit by the sun and moon
in the beauty of each daily sunrise and sunset.
Even the rainbow stretching across the sky reveals
the vast extent and expanse Your word covers.
How then can we measure the praise due to You
our Awesome God.
Amen.

ABOVE AND BEYOND

2 Chronicles 6:14,18

Lord God, nothing and no-one in heaven or on earth can compare to You in either authority or power. Even the heavens cannot contain Your glory but spill it down upon the earth for us to behold.
Daily, Your eyes seek out Your own upon the earth for You have made each one of us the living temples of the Holy Spirit.
You have engraved Your name upon us and set us apart for Your purposes.
Come, Holy Spirit, and break down any mindsets or barriers we have built, unaware, within our hearts and minds that prevent You from receiving the praise and worship You are due.
Hear our prayers Father as we seek to advance Your Kingdom and magnify the name of Your Son, Jesus.
Hear the cries of our repentant hearts, forgive our sins and make us whole.
Amen.

MIRACULOUS MOVEMENT

Psalm 76:4, Psalm 77:13,14

Who is as great as You, our God?
You are the God who does wonders among the
people who testify and declare Your strength and
power to save.
Likewise, the elements acknowledge Your
authority: seas part, clouds guide, winds become
still, the earth shakes and lightning lights up the
skies at Your word.
Your authority is both seen and heard
from the heavens, creating great fear among man
as You reveal Yourself as God.
Who then may stand in Your presence? For Your
glory covers Your mountain and Your vision is
more excellent than the sight of any bird of prey.
Your Word magnifies and illuminates Your ways
bringing life and a clearer vision of Your
sovereignty to the believer.
You take great joy in the praises of Your children
and like a banner You cover them with love.
Amen.

KING OF HEAVEN

Psalm 32, Psalm 33, Psalm 147

I will praise You, Lord. I will speak of the
wonders of Your everlasting Kingdom of Glory.
I will declare Your greatness and Your mighty
power for You have set Your throne within the
heavens and hosts of angels wait to do Your
bidding.
Your eyes remain fixed upon Your people. Your
gaze never falters or turns from us for Your joy is
to teach and instruct us in the way we should go.
Lord, You look down from heaven daily to observe
and consider all our ways for You have fashioned
each heart individually to reflect and reveal the
greatness of Your love.
Amen.

UNLIMITED GLORY

John 3:16

Father God, I will look to You alone as my helper,
my source of strength and provision.
Your presence is always by my side. You know
every intricate detail of my life; see everything I
do; and yet Your love is limitless towards me.
As the great creator who spoke all things into
being. You have breathed Your life into me.
You move daily in unseen mysterious ways to
bring about Your purposes in my life.
How can I not stand in awe and wonder when I
think of how You sent Your son into the world to
rescue me?
How can I not be moved by the sacrifice He made
in trading the glory of Heaven for earth and his
royal home for a simple stable?
How can I not praise when I think of how He
gave his life over to death before rising from the
dead in a glorious, resurrected form?
Now He reigns on a throne beside You, seated
at Your right hand in the heavens waiting to
return to earth again.
Amen.

GENERATION RISING

Acts 2:17

O Lord, the force of Your power and the value of
Your wisdom is beyond measure.
From generation to generation Your name has
been honoured and Your purposes revered.
In Your anger You break strongholds
and bring false idols crashing down for Your one
desire is that we should seek You and find You.
You long to bless us with the knowledge of who
You are that we might encounter the greatness of
Your love towards us.
It is for this reason that You have promised to
show Yourself anew through Your word, through
parables and through the miraculous work of
Your hands both in natural and supernatural
events.
Father God, we cry out for You to do these things
again and bring a great revival here on earth.
Amen.

IMMEASURABLE WORTH

Job 28:12, 24-28, Proverbs 9:10.

Father, all the wisdom we need to walk within the
power of Your ways is found in You.
Your vision spreads to the very ends of the earth
as You search for those who can be established for
Your purposes and shoulder the weight of the
Holy Spirit's mantle.
To every person You have given a measure of
Your life, for Your laws determine both the
seasons for the rains of refreshing and which
course of life will incur Your judgement.
Everything which is hidden is brought into Your
light and exposed to Your sight.
Modern man does not know or recognise the
value of Your wisdom but those with eyes to see
and ears to hear place its value higher than the
price of rubies.
For such to enter the fear of the Lord is to enter
the highest place honour and to acknowledge who
You are as God is to enter a new life of
understanding, where evil is no more.
I will praise Your holy name.
Amen.

DECLARATIONS OF THE HEART

Job 37:23-24, Psalm 34:8.

The greatness of Your majesty, O God, is revealed
in the Heavenly realms alone, for it is so mighty in
splendour that our mortal minds cannot imagine
nor grasp it.
The excellence of Your judgement and the
abundance of Your justice is evident for You
show no partiality but call all to look upon You
and open their heart to Your words.
You have put Your wisdom into the minds of
those who seek You and given understanding to
the hearts of those who trust in You.
Daily, You put Your words into our mouths
that we might speak of Your wonderful ways as
our Father and the mighty blessings You put in
our paths. Our eyes see and our mouths declare
Your goodness for each dawn is rich with new
promises.
You are always near to us, O God, to give us help
and show Your strength
in every circumstance.
Amen.

ANTHEMS OF ADORATION

Revelation 19:16

As King of kings and Lord of lords Your name is
holy. At the very mention of Your name, the
angels bow down to worship and adore You.
How much more then do You delight in the true
worship of Your own people when, led by the
Spirit, they testify to Your truth?
As spirit beings who live in an earthly body, teach
us by Your Holy Spirit how to honour You with
our thoughts, desires, and emotions that we might
be in the world, but not of it.
Father help us to give ourselves wholly over to
You without needing to count the cost, that we
might partner with You in Your vision, and see
that doing Your will alone is a rich reward.
Amen.

THE SWEETEST DESIRE

Psalm 19, Ephesians 4:16

Lord Your glorious heavenly language is written in the mysteries of the starry skies, for in the secrets of their origins, Your master plan for salvation is displayed. Daily creation utters revelations of You in their own individual speech whilst night after night You offer the invitation to deepen our knowledge of You by seeking revelation. Yes, there is not one form of speech or language, heavenly or earthly, where Your voice cannot be heard. Every language is connected and so the spoken mysteries of who You are have seamlessly gone out to the very ends of the earth. The revelation of Your divine laws, the testimonies hidden within Your statutes, the treasures to be found in Your commandments, the sweet delights found within fear of the Lord and the open invitation hidden within Your judgements are more to be desired than base gold. Yes, to taste the truth in Your words is to taste something sweeter than the fresh honey from the honeycomb for every word is a reminder of Your love by which You will build Your body for Your purposes here on earth. Amen.

THE MIND OF CHRIST

1 Corinthians 2:16, Philippians 2:2-5

Lord, who could presume to know Your mind
that they could stand and instruct You?
Your thoughts are beyond our understanding for
Your vision is sourced in the truth of who You are.
You are love. Every action You perform is good.
Every choice You make is righteous.
What greater example of the Father's heart can
there be than how You chose to suffer on our
behalf through the death of Your only Son, Jesus?
You sent him to earth to set us free from our own
self-centredness so that, through the Holy Spirit,
we might learn to have a compassionate concern
for others without being competitive or combative
in heart.
Father, teach us how to be co-operative with
others, having a positive attitude towards those
around us that we might unite with people and
reveal to others the thoughts You hold towards
them. Thank You for the strength and
transforming power of the Holy Spirit by whom
You show Your unconditional love day by day.
Amen.

SEEKING SERVANTS

2 Chronicles 16:9

Almighty God You look down from the heavens
with a fervent desire to find those whose only
focus, and passionate desire, is set on finding You.
You have promised to show Your strength to
those who are devoted to understanding the
wisdom in Your word and what it reveals about
Your power.
Without the Holy Spirit's revelation, anything we
think about or connect to Your words is proved to
be limited and produces nothing.
For Your desires to come into being on this earth,
for the reality of Heaven to invade our daily lives,
we ask for a heavenly perspective of Your ways.
Help us, Holy Spirit, to live day by day
under Your anointing and in obedience to Your
prompting that we might be protected from the
snares of deceit and lies. and established in the
truth of Your holiness.
Amen.

STRONG AND SECURE

Psalm 23, John 14:18, 2 Corinthians 1:3

Lord, help me to find comfort in Your reality as
my heavenly Father.
Take my hand and lead me into the stillness of the
secret place of prayer where my soul will be
refreshed by Your life-giving words.
Teach me to trust in the reality that every detail of
my life is not hidden from You; that You can and
will provide a way for me to walk boldly into each
day knowing You are with me and for me in all
things.
Capture my gaze and deeply root me in the
knowledge of Your love that I might advance
through every trial and stand firm in every form
of opposition knowing Your love is everlasting
and Your victory will be glorious!
Come to me afresh in Your power Holy Spirit.
Teach me what it means to live as a royal child of
God.
I will praise You, Lord, for Your faithfulness is
everlasting. From the beginning to the end of my
life, Your words will be my source of security and
they will direct my path. Amen.

38

WAY MAKER

Exodus 14:16, Joshua 6:5, James 1:17

Lord, who is stronger or more powerful than You
when it comes to defending and leading Your
people?
You are quick to break down every wall that
hinders their purpose, and to part the seas that
they might enter Your promises.
When You speak to an obstacle, it has to move.
Whatever You put Your hand to cannot be
changed or reversed.
Throughout the ages and generations, from the
beginning of time until our present day, Your
Word and hand has made paths for us to draw
closer to You; and Your Word will continue to
mould and shape our futures both on this earth
and for eternity.
When we consider Your goodness and the
perfection of Your ways as our Heavenly Father,
our eyes are opened to how vain, transitory, and
temporary the things of this world really are.
Every morning You greet us with fresh favour and
forgiveness; with arms always open for us to turn
from the shadows and run into Your loving
embrace. Amen.

COVERED

Deuteronomy 33:26, Psalm 86:11

In majesty and splendour, You ride Your chariot across the Heavens, and gaze upon the earth as our eternal King.
Your hands are swift to take up Your bow and sword and lead Your angelic armies to war on our behalf. Your strength never fails, Your words never miss their target, Your victory is inevitable.
It is Your very greatness as our Champion defender that assures us that at any time, we can run to You and find refuge and safety in the presence of Your love.
Teach us the reality of this truth, Lord, that we might grasp the full power of Your love and passionate jealousy over us. Help us to unite our hearts to the surety of Your authority and reject the circling voices of fear that so easily beset our lives. Lend Your strength to us, O Lord, as we seek You out as a mighty Warrior.
Teach us how to serve You through adoration and praise; how speaking of Your mighty works releases Your power and presence in creation, like an unstoppable tide flowing in and out.
Teach us to rest in You. Amen.

OF TIME AND TIMES

Psalm 31:15, 2 Timothy 3, 2 Peter 3:8

God, Your reality as Father is an everlasting truth, not limited to the confines of cultures of time. We live by the measure of minutes and hours recorded within every day, but to You time is non-existent, for Your realm is eternal.

Help us to surrender our concept of time to embrace the availability of Your unlimited power as God.

Lord, Your Word speaks of perilous times when we will have to choose between embracing Your eternal perspective and reality as God, or yielding to the seduction of pride, self-dependence, worldly pleasures, and materialism as our source of security. Help us to make the right choice and not substitute the joy to be found in intimate relationship with You for a mere knowledge of You that denies Your authority and power.

May Your inspired words of truth, the reality of Your position as our living King and Redeemer and the indwelling and overflowing power of the Holy Spirit continuously work within us as we are changed into Your image to the glory of Your name. Amen.

BLOSSOMING RELATIONSHIP

Isaiah 61:11, Hosea 10:12, Luke 8:11

Almighty, awesome God, by Your word and the
strength of Your hand, the earth brings forth new
buds of blossoming life.
When I gaze upon the garden, I am in awe at how
You cause the vast variety of seeds sown to burst
forth in their various seasons.
In the same way, You instruct us by Your words,
calling us to sow righteousness that we might reap
a harvest of steadfast love.
Break up the fallow ground within our hearts,
Lord, and cause us to seek You with fresh fervour.
Nurture us as we grow within Your life and begin
to take on our true form in righteousness.
Lord, every word You speak to us is seed that
gives us the strength to put down deep roots and
find in You, life in abundance.
You are our source, Lord Jesus, teach us what it
means to live in active intimate relationship with
You that we might bring forth much fruit in our
lives to the glory of Your name.
Amen

TREASURE IN CLAY JARS

Genesis 1:27, Genesis 2:7, 2 Corinthians 4:7

Father God, it was Your desire to finish off the
masterpiece of Your creation by setting at its
centre the living breathing image of Yourself.
Your fingers wetted, moved, and sculpted the dust
of the ground until You had created an intricately
designed form with the capacity to hold Your life
and move within it. You breathed Your own life
into the stunning, hollow sculpture You called
'man' and before Your eyes he became a living
being.
As an earthen vessel You designed and created
him
to carry the treasures of Your heart and adorned
him in Your glorious light. This rich treasure of
knowing You in Your glory goes far above and
beyond our mortal limitations and understanding,
and yet Your glory is still seen upon and within
us, shining within our hearts.
How then can we doubt Your reality or reject You
when our lives revolve around Your power, Your
breath of life within us? Lord, cleanse us by the
power of Your blood, restore our faith and make
us worthy of our calling. Amen.

VOICES IN THE WIND

Exodus 10:19, Exodus 10 & 14, Job 37:17,
Solomon 4:16,
Psalm 148:8, Jeremiah 51:16

Almighty God, Your power is made known through the force of the unseen wind; for by its voice both in gentle whispering breeze and howling gale Your mighty acts are spoken of across the earth.
Each of the four winds have different capacities by which they show Your wonders, O Lord.
They are a treasure bestowed upon us from the Heavenly storehouses to bring us into greater revelation of who You are as God.
The tempestuous stormy wind of the East is a promise that You will fulfil Your words of judgement, whilst the quiet wind of the South is a promise that You will lead us into Your rest.
The strong wind of the north declares Your hand of deliverance whilst the dancing wind of the west offers fresh hope of restoration.
Lord, let Your winds blow upon and within our lives that we may know You better and in listening to their separate voices, learn to listen and be obedient to Your own. Amen.

ALL SEEING, ALL KNOWING

Nehemiah 9:6, Psalm 9:4, Romans 1:20

Lord God, You sit enthroned in the heavens and at Your command the sprawling tapestry of creation is laid out before Your eyes.
All that is living is revealed to Your sight. Your power runs through their veins and each microscopic detail in their DNA is inscribed with Your word. In their lives, Your invisible attributes as God are clearly seen, and all of them understand that they were created by Your eternal power for the pleasure of the Godhead.
Why then do we believe that we have an excuse to deny Your incorruptible glory as our Lord and God? It was by Your word the heavens came into existence, angelic legions were summoned into being and the earth was re-granted its form and filled with life as the flood waters fled at Your command.
You are the greater sustainer and preserver of life and as such the entire host of Heaven worships You. Let us also, as those spoken and breathed into being and moulded into Your image, give You the glory You are rightfully due. Amen.

PRAISING IN YOUR PRESENCE

Isaiah 40:4 -5, Romans 5:8, Hebrews 13:5

O Lord my God, how amazing are Your ways.
From the days we spend on the heights of Your
mountain to the times spent in depths of the
valley of despair, there is always a reason for Your
name to be praised.
No-one compares to You, as the High King of
heaven, for the sound of Your voice thunders for
our attention and bring us, as Your children, back
into alignment.
Sometimes Your voice takes on a gentle whisper
bringing us encouragement and the reassurance
that You are an ever present help in times of
trouble.
It is against Your nature and character to leave us
to face our trials alone for we hold rich value in
Your sight as those dearly loved and worth the
sacrifice
of Your Son, Jesus.
By His resurrection we were given Your life. Now
by the Holy Spirit You live in and through us and
take us deeper into our journey of faith.
Amen.

GARMENTS OF GRACE

Psalm 51:10, Jeremiah 10:23

God, the majestic wonder of Your royal garments
of glory, grace and holiness are beyond all human
description.
To gaze upon Your magnificence as King,
enthroned in the heavens, is to enter deeper
wonder at the mystery of how we are made in
Your image.
Yet Your greatest longing is for us to know You
and intimately love You as we recognise the
extent of Your favour and mercy towards us
throughout the ages.
Without You, we are, and we have, nothing. There
is nothing we can do outside of being dependent
upon You in some way for it is You who directs
our steps in life.
Lord, expose to us our need to constantly yield to
You and to depend upon You as our source of
strength that You might purify our hearts and
create in us a joy and commitment to Your vision
and purposes.
Amen.

BURNING WORDS

Psalm 135:7, Jeremiah 20:96, Matthew 5:16,
John 20:22

Your authority, O Lord, will endure forever, for
Your greatness and power goes far above and
beyond any other idol or image of a god that man
has created. They have fallen into the dust, yet
You remain living and enthroned on high.
I will surrender to Your authority Lord; I will
pour out heartfelt words of praise and adoration. I
will honour You and enthrone You by declaring
the value and richness of who You are in my life.
Blow upon my heart, Holy Spirit, like a pure wind
of fire. Speak to me and engrave Your words into
my heart.
Just as You breathed on the disciples, breath on
me that I might receive You afresh, Holy Spirit.
Teach me to speak the language of the Father that
I might speak life to those within my community
and among those You place in my path.
May the light of the life You have placed within
me, shine to the glory of Your name.
Amen

THE NARROW PATH

John 7:29, John 14

Lord, when Your son Jesus walked amongst us
on the earth, he took on Your name as 'I AM' and
revealed Your greatness in our eyes.
We learnt to find our way in life by the words of
Your truth and so enter the fullness of all that You
are and all that You had promised.
We learnt to recognise and embrace You as our
Heavenly Father by encountering Your reality in
the lifestyle and words of Your son.
We started to gain new insight into Your heart,
thoughts, emotions and desires by watching them
being lived out before our eyes.
Little by little, we came to know You and to walk
amidst the Kingdom of Heaven that Your son
brought upon the earth.
Thank You, Father, for revealing Yourself to me
that I might see the true nature of Your life and
goodness through the sacrificial love of Your Son.
Lord may my life reflect You in the same measure
as I surrender afresh to becoming obedient to
Your will. Amen.

RIVERS OF LIFE

John 4:10

Lord, as I gaze upon creation, the sheer beauty
and vastness of Your glory overwhelms me.
From the tiniest blade of grass to the rich canopy
of the mighty oak tree, the greatness of Your
handiwork is evident in its detail.
Father, thank You for refreshing rain that You
send from heaven to satisfy the trees and plants
and to bring forth life.
You are the true and living water that satisfies our
thirst. You invite us to drink deeply of Your life-
giving words that we might become living wells
and storehouses for those yet to come that they
also might rise and step into Your everlasting life.
I praise You for the water of life that You give for I
know without it, everything would die.
Thank You also for the water of baptism that
leads us out of death and into life as we are
cleansed, made whole and given a new identity in
You.
Amen.

THE POWER OF PRAYER

Psalm 139, Proverbs 1:23

Lord God, every promise found in Your word is rich in wisdom and full of the power of the Holy Spirit.
Make Your words known to me that I might embrace You as my Father and begin to understand the mystery of the fear of the Lord.
As I start this journey of seeking the truth of Your word in the secret place of prayer, lead me deeper into a posture of humility that my heart and my motives might be pure before Your sight.
Only then will I find the boldness to come before Your throne and make my supplications known; for Your ears are sensitive only to the righteous words birthed from a broken heart.
Lord You see my heart, there is nothing within me that is not exposed to Your sight.
Come, Holy Spirit, and remove anything from my life that displeases You.
Amen.

UNSHAKEABLE FOUNDATIONS

Philippians 2:10-11

Lord, Your Kingdom is founded on the greatness
of Your power and the supreme glory of Your
authority.
There is no-one who can stand in Your presence,
for Your gaze and Your power penetrates all, and
brings all who come before You to their knees as
they acknowledge Your sovereignty and Lordship.
Father, the power of Your authority is still seen
in the works You perform and the words You
speak upon the earth.
Even in these days, You have shaken the
foundations and structures that have built our
nation, and revealed the vanity of those things we
placed our security in within this world.
You have made it abundantly clear that whatever
is not built upon You will not stand; for
You are our only safe and sure foundation, the
rock on which we should be building our lives.
You alone are the mighty, powerful God
in whom we should place our trust.
Amen.

THE PRESENCE OF POWER

Psalm 8:1-9, Psalm 19:1-4, Psalm 66:5, Romans 1:18-20

Lord, I am constantly overcome with awe and
wonder when I gaze up at the night sky and
behold the stars and vastness of the heavens.
My heart is filled with new songs of praise as I
think upon You and how You sought to save me
that I might begin to know You as God.
Every detail of the heavens shouts down to the
earth of Your greatness, and that You alone
deserve the glory. I will praise You, mighty God,
for in Your great mercy, You make Your presence,
peace, and power available to us each day. You are
constantly interested in our lives and daily
command Your angels to watch over us and guard
us as those who are Your own.
Thank You for the remarkable gift of Your Holy
Spirit who ministers to us Your words, both with
discipline and with comfort, as You lead us in all
truth.
Father, may my life be a pleasing sacrifice before
You and a living testimony of Your great love for
me.
Amen.

LIFE SPOKEN FORTH

John 1:1, John 4:24, John 10:10

Father God, every word You speak is eternally
recorded, written, and brought to pass, therefore
it is impossible for any to fade from existence, or
be prevented in their purpose.
You revealed the power of Your words to bring life
through the life Your son. Throughout His
ministry, He operated in the spiritual and natural
realm; declaring the Word of God to those who
came to seek Him.
Every word He spoke, He revealed the fullness of
Your truth and life, accompanying them with
signs and wonders that put an end to doubt and
unbelief.
Father, I thank You for those You have placed in
positions of authority today who are building
Your Kingdom by surrendering their lives to
worship You in spirit and in truth, and to lead,
guide and emulate the love and ways of God to us
on the earth.
Amen.

BOLDLY COME

Hebrews 4:16

Lord, when we gaze upon You, we are in awe of
Your greatness and the power of Your sovereignty
as the King of Kings and Lord of Lords.
Yet in Your great mercy and love, You openly
invite us to approach You with our own petitions
and to intercede to You on behalf of others.
Without the sacrifice of Your Son, such access to
Your Throne and mercy would never have been
possible, for being holy You could not look on sin
without bringing judgement upon it.
Jesus, by becoming the image of sin and
sacrificing His life for us on the cross, lifted that
image of sin from us by washing us in His own
blood that we might be seen as His image and
become pure in Your sight.
Lord, I thank You that through His great love for
me, I can now come close to You and speak with
You knowing that You hear my prayers.
Thank You for those You have answered
and for those waiting to be answered.
Amen.

NOBODY LIKE YOU

Genesis 1:27, Revelation 4:8-11

Lord, You dwell in the splendour of the Heavens.
Your voice is like the powerful roar of the thunder
during a violent storm. Your strength is like a
lightning bolt that splits and divides mountains.
Is it any wonder that the nations shake before
Your display of sovereign power and authority for
they know that no-one and nothing can equal
You?!
Even in the greatness of Your sovereignty You
never fail to show Your love, mercy, and
faithfulness towards us being fully deserving of all
our praise, worship, and honour.
Before the sight and revelation of Your holiness
as our creator and Lord, what are we that You
would focus Your every thought and attention
upon us? What are we that You would choose to
bestow upon us Your own image, wrap us in Your
own glorious garments of grace and draw us
closer to Your heart in sincere love?
Before such love we can only surrender and give
to You our all.
Amen

SURROUNDED BY HOPE

Isaiah 41:10

Father God, You speak Your life-giving words
directly into my heart, driving away any hold that
circumstances and trials may have on me and
replacing my fears with the comfort of Your
continuous presence.
I thank You, for I see throughout my life that You
have never left me to face things alone or
abandoned me when things got tough. Instead,
You brought people around me, as both friends
and as a family to love, encourage and to pray
together
in times of happiness, difficulty, sickness and
celebrational joy.
You have always been in my life and even now
You are walking beside me in faithfully sharing
Your vision, speaking mysteries to my heart, and
daily bringing me hope, for I know Your powerful
love displayed in and through my life can never be
overcome.
Amen.

FATHER OF THE FATHERLESS

Jeremiah 32:19

God, the greatness of Your love and mercy
towards me astounds me.
Thank You for listening to the cries of my heart
as I ask You to intercede and responding with the
wisdom of Your comforting counsel and the
outworking of Your power in my life.
I know that nothing asked for, out of a loving
heart, is too hard for You to answer.
You hear the cry of a baby.
You listen to those whose hearts are broken.
Your compassion is moved into action on behalf
of the orphan and the widow.
You stand with those who know You
and love You.
You long for those in darkness
to come into Your open arms.
Lord, I come to You, I love You.
Amen.

DESIRED AND DIRECTED

Psalm 1

Lord, You are intricately involved in every detail
of our lives, for Your greatest desire is that we
might learn and understand what it means to be
righteous in Your sight.
Daily Your eyes and ears are open to our
progress, and You search our hearts and minds
that You might mentor us and give us a greater
revelation of who You are.
You walk with us in every detail of our lives,
seeing all, yet still offering us Your hand as a
means of provision, as You seek to lead us out of
our troubles and despair into a place of trust and
rest in Your great love.
Lord, open our eyes to Your continuous presence,
Your loving voice and the leading of Your Spirit in
everything we face. Become our only focus, our
only desire, that the power of Your Holy Spirit
might be at work in and through our lives at this
time and bring forth a great harvest of souls for
Your glory.
Amen

A GREATER VISION

Isaiah 2, Revelation 4

Lord, Your name is established in the high places;
Your authority is exalted above the mountains
and the hills.
Father, when You call us in the secret place of
prayer, our spirit ascends into the Heavenly
places to be with You and to wait upon Your
commands.
Like Your servant, John, You invite us to enter
Your holy presence, before the Throne, that You
might show us everything that must take place in
the times to come.
As such, You call us to walk and live within these
higher places of revelation and increasing depths
of intimate relationship with You.
Daily You offer to open the treasures in Your
word to us that we may see You, our mighty and
mysterious God in all Your power and glory.
Bring us ever nearer to the very heart
of who You are.
Amen.

HEAVENLY PROVISION

Psalm 145:8-9, Psalm 148

I want to praise and declare the excellence of
Your name, O God, for Your name is the door
through which Your glory is witnessed.
The authority within Your name is greater than
any other authority on earth or in heaven.
As we set our gaze upon You daily, You prove
Yourself to be the source and provision of all our
needs. Forgive us then for the times when we
received Your provision but ceased to recognise
You as the source, believing them to be merely
daily supports for our own needs and desires.
Let us never forget that You can choose to close
Your hand and deprive mankind from knowing
Your goodness, that we might recognise the
extent of our rebellious works and repent of the
doubtful words we've used against You.
As the judge of the whole earth, You choose how
and when to give what belongs to You. Yet even
when we anger You with our pride, Your great
mercy and compassion towards us remains.
As our Father, Your faithfulness and greatness
leave us in awe. Amen

SALVATION'S SONG

Isaiah 5:12

Lord, the greatness of Your power and authority is
worthy of the highest forms of praise, for it is only
through You that everything in Heaven and Earth
continues to exist, move, and bring forth life.
Jesus, You demonstrated the life-giving nature of
Your power by showing us Your desire to save and
redeem us from the power of death and bring us
back into relationship with You.
At the very beginning of time this great plan of
salvation was discussed, drawn out and agreed
upon between the Godhead.
It was spoken of and recorded throughout Your
Word from beginning to end that we might
understand the extent of Your great love for us.
As the seed of the tree of life that sprung from the
line of David, as the promised Messiah, You,
Jesus allowed yourself to fall to the hold of death
that new life would spring forth to all who
recognised You for who You really are.
In Your Words are found the fruit of resurrection
life, and under the covering of Your presence,
power is fully restored.
Amen.

ABIDING FRUITFULNESS

Isaiah 5:12

Father, You have set us apart to be Your very own.
Like vines growing on a hillside, Your purpose for
each of our lives is to bear and bring forth sweet
and luscious fruit that will make up a new wine- a
new expression of Your glory.
It is for this reason that You love, nurture and
protect us as Your very own, yet even now we are
quick to ignore Your presence and power in our
lives and remain blind to the work You are doing
within us.
Lord, Your heart is to bring us into partnership
with Your plans and purpose that we might glorify
Your name and find joy in honouring and serving
You.
Set our focus completely on You, Lord. Forgive us
for going our own way and putting ourselves first.
Let us humbly recognise the truth that
without You, we have nothing and are nothing
and choose to show You our heartfelt gratitude for
Your daily love and mercy.
Amen.

CHOSEN TO RULE AND REIGN.

Psalm 24

As the Commander of Angel Armies each one present recognises that the power and authority are Yours, and Yours alone. In the same way You raise up leaders on this earth who will recognise Your rulership and reign and commit to a life of obedience that Your will might be done.

You call many to arms but of those assembled only a few possess the heart and character needed to become leaders. For many the strength of Your divine commands as our Commander have been lost; for those who have been entrusted with Your words have diluted them and made them weak.

Who then will You raise up to be a pure clear powerful voice to the nations?

Who amongst Your own has a heart that is pure and a reputation for having words, motives and actions that are uncompromised and undefiled? Only those completely surrendered to Your will, who walk in obedience to Your instructions, will be granted the privilege of being entrusted with Your authority to prepare the way for You as King.

Amen.

HELD IN HIS HANDS

Psalm 24:1-2

God, I am in awe of the wonders and miracles You
perform.
When I look on the stars, I think about how Your
hands positioned them in space.
When I look upon creation, I marvel at how You
clothed the earth in beauty.
When I see a newborn baby, I am taken aback by
the intricate craftmanship of its form and
overwhelmed by the idea that You formed this
tiny miracle within its mother's womb.
I look upon Your nail scarred hands and think of
how they healed the sick and raised the dead; of
their strength in parting the sea and opening the
earth.
Your hands are kind hands, for I remember how
You tenderly touched the eyes of the blind
that they might see again.
Those hands still reach out to everyone in
invitation as You call them to walk with You.
I know Your hands will never let me go, for with
You I am safe and secure.
Amen.

GENERATION TO GENERATION

Genesis 22:17, Psalm 139:18

God, the evidence of Your power and glory can be seen shining forth in the phenomenal details of the natural world. The closer we look at these testimonies of You, the more we realise that You are beyond our comprehension and understanding.
When I stand quietly by the shoreline and gaze on the ever-changing hues of the sea, the brightness of the sun and the radiant golden tones of the sand, I think on You and hear You speaking.
The brightness and warmth of the sun reminds me of Your divine power.
The countless grains of sand remind me that Your promises cannot be altered but remain from generation upon generation.
When I think of how the sea tides move endlessly both by day and night, I am reminded of how eternity is held in Your hands.
I am daily in awe of You, my amazing God and how You speak and move in both hearts and lives.
Amen.

UNFAILING LOVE

John 1:3, 1 Thessalonians 5:21

Father God, You have made a way for me to
approach You by embracing Your words of truth
and living by the leading of Your Holy Spirit.
Now when I look on the world around me, I see
all things as being made by Your hand, and I give
You praise for them all.
How intricate is Your vision and how
knowledgeable Your mind when it comes to
seeing and knowing the heart of that which You
have created! Even when our own hearts turn,
You are swift to pursue us, for Your great love and
mercy towards us means You will never give up.
Come, Holy Spirit, cleanse the thoughts of our
hearts, inspire us and direct us to go deeper into
relationship with You that we might know You
and give You the praise and honour You are due.
In Your faithfulness, Lord reveal to us the
greatness of Your wisdom daily that we might
begin to see our lives with an eternal perspective.
Let us hold fast to Your goodness and grace as we
honour You by serving all.
Amen.

THE DAY OF THE LORD

1 Thessalonians 5:2

Lord, in Your great knowledge, You have
established a day when Your power and glory will
be revealed upon the earth.
I know, in my spirit, that the Day is fast
approaching when the mighty strength of Your
hand will move in judgement against everything
that has been built or created that was not of You.
when Your hand of judgement strikes.
Idols and man-made materialism will stripped
away and those things that have taken Your place
will be removed.
Like a mighty flood, Your power and Spirit will
move upon this earth and those who have turned
from Your words and rejected Your warnings
will perish.
Therefore, in Your mercy teach us to wait upon
You, to listen and activate the teachings
You place in our hearts day by day that we might
see You and live
Amen.

CARRIED INTO THE TRUTH

Psalm 91:11

Heavenly Father, You love us so much that You
have ordered Your angelic warriors to watch over
us and protect us. As heavenly soldiers under
Your command, they act according to Your word
alone, bringing Your words directly from the
Throne room to our hearts in the secret place of
prayer.
Teach us to pay attention to their specific
instructions when it comes to knowing what You
desire; for Your will to be done that the glory
might be given to Your name.
Your Kingdom is established on the power and
the glory of Your authority, and it is Your desire
that we, on earth, respond to You as King in the
same way that the Heavenly host do.
They recognise the pure, uncompromised power
of Your words and honour You as God for they
understand the freedom that each word of Truth
can bring from the hold of sin and slavery.
Thank You, Lord for revealing the extent of Your
great love, and for establishing our freedom
through Jesus' death on the cross.
Amen.

TRANSFORMATION

Jeremiah 10:6

You alone are worthy of our praise Lord for nothing, and no-one, can compare to You, either in the Heavens, or on the earth.
Your banner of authority is lifted high above the nations and the glorious power of Your Heavenly army is greater than any force or power that can be mustered on the earth.
Daily You reveal Yourself to people worldwide and rejoice as their lives are changed by turning back to You.
You delight in showing Your creativity in miraculous healings and wonders, putting to shame the powers of darkness that have held people captive in confusion and fear.
With violence You break the strongholds of idol worship and addiction that have blinded hearts and minds to the reality of who You are, and with tenderness You restore sight to the spiritually blind
and hearing to the spiritually deaf.
Move in our nation and nations of the world and declare to them the reality that Your return, here on earth, is imminent. Amen.

THE SONG OF THE SAVIOUR

Psalm 92, Isaiah 9, Zephaniah 3:17

Father God, You delight to move among us and enter every detail of our daily lives by Your strength and power. You take great delight in Your children and show the extent of Your great love by offering forgiveness to those who ask with heartfelt longing to be restored to You.

Daily You sing over us with deep emotion finding ever increasing joy in removing the hold of sin over us and reclothing us in garments of grace and glory. It only takes one person's hearts cry to move Your heart in response, to awaken Your great love and stir You to establish justice as the true Judge of all the earth.

Your judgement and justice are eternal for not one letter of Your word can be removed, replaced, or altered to change its purpose or stop it from coming to pass. Your anger is not easily pacified, but even then, You still stretch out Your hand in mercy with the desire that Your words will come to pass. Even in Your chastisement You long for us to reveal our need of You that You might show us mercy.

Amen.

SHADES OF PROVISION

Lamentations 3:23, Romans 8:35, Hebrews 13:5

God, the sheer scale of Your might and authority makes it impossible to think that You would ever turn away from Your word or Your faithfulness to us day by day.

Everything I have needed in my life has been received from Your gracious hand for You enjoy revealing Your goodness to me as I wait upon You in prayer.

When I ponder Your magnificence as God, it drives me to seek Your heart further and examine the reality of my own thoughts, motives and actions before You.

Your exposure of the deepest thoughts of my heart drives me to come before You and bow in sincere repentance at Your feet.

I know that Your love for me is not dependant on me but is the very essence of who You are. It is You who chooses not to reject or leave me but to pursue my adoration and my love forever.

Amen.

THE GRACIOUS GIFT GIVER

John 16:13

God, as our Heavenly Father, it is Your desire
that we embrace the great love You have towards
us as Your children.
You long to guide and lead us deeper into
understanding the wisdom in Your words and the
power of truth that they hold.
Every word that You have spoken holds the
answer to every question or difficulty we might
face in life. As such, they are Your gift to each one
of us, to help us discern what it really means to
belong to You as Your child. You sent us the Holy
Spirit as our comforter and minister, teacher, and
helper. Through Him we learn that You are ever
present with us, living on the inside of every
believer.
Father, help us to know our identity in Your
family and to live in the knowledge that we bear
Your name, are precious in Your sight and are
totally loved by You.
Amen.

CALM IN THE STORM

Psalm 4:6-10, Philippians 4:6-8, Hebrews 4.

Father, You alone are our source of peace and rest
amid the chaos and turmoil in our world.
If we take the time to listen, we will hear You
speaking to our hearts, calling us to reside in the
stillness of Your presence and focus upon Your
awesome power as God.
As God, You operate outside of the confines and
expectations of time that we live in, and therefore
You long for us to set aside special times of quiet
where we can be alone with You.
How vital are these times when it comes to
learning to know You: to speak with You, enquire
of You and to honour and worship You for who
You are.
These are the promised times of rest You have
invited all Your children to enter: an invitation to
to put aside every distraction that wages war
against our mind and to simply rest in Your
presence knowing that listening to and applying
Your words of truth will bring the victory in every
situation we face and lead us into peace.
Amen.

WONDERFUL WORDS

Psalm 77:19, Job 38:4

Lord, the precise details and blueprints behind the wonders You performed on the earth remain a mystery to us.
When You allow the blessings You have poured out upon our life to be removed even for a little while, we start doubting Your reasoning. When we face agony and despair, we are quick to ask why You created us and start doubting our purpose in life.
Lord teach us, once more, the lessons that You taught Job: how Your hand is always upon us and Your presence remains ever nearby.
Speak to us the same words of power and glory that You spoke to him. Restore our faith and lead us into an even greater degree trust in You that at the end of our trial we might receive the reward of the lavish blessings You seek to pour out upon us.
Let our testimony of You, like Job's testimony of You as his living Redeemer, become our constant source of praise and the daily song from our lips.
Amen.

FAITHFUL AND TRUE

Psalm 31:19, Proverbs 8:13

Lord, You hear every voice that calls to You and,
in Your faithfulness, You make haste to draw near
and respond in Your power.
Forgive us for listening to the voice of fear and
choosing to carry the burden of all the anxieties
placed upon us instead of trusting You.
Help us recognise Your sovereign authority and
power over all things as Lord, that we might come
humbly before You and sit at Your feet.
Teach us the fear of the Lord that we might begin
to walk in and live out Your words of wisdom.
Father, may we always be grateful for the power
and invitation to prayer that You give to all Your
saints that You might respond in grace and favour
and move in every aspect of our lives.
Amen.

GOODNESS REVEALED

Isaiah 66:2, Romans 1:20, James 1:17

God, the beauty of Your craftmanship as the
Master Creator leaves me in awe.
The touch of hand brought all things into being
giving them shape, detail, and form.
From the very beginning, You have found
immense joy in Your work as a Creator.
Ever since the creation of the earth, You have
delighted in making sure Your invisible attributes,
eternal power and divine nature are clearly seen
in everything we look upon.
The beauty and intricate detail found in every
tree,
leaf and flower were hand fashioned and crafted
by You to catch our attention and focus.
You also created us in Your own image,
and equipped us with the ability to express in
constructive and creative ways, that we might
bring further honour and glory to Your name.
When I ponder that truth, I am convinced
beyond measure that You are good, and I
humbly receive Your perfect gifts for I know
that You will not change. Amen.

THE HEARTBEAT OF GOD

Joel 37:23-24, 2 Chronicles 16:9

God, You are awesome, almighty, and majestic,
yet You shroud Yourself in mystery so that we
cannot find You in our own strength but are led
into deeper decrees of faith and trust.
By faith, You reveal the excellence of power both
to bring judgement, to secure justice and to
release abundant life.
You do not desire to oppress anyone, for when it
comes to those You have made, You have no
partiality, nor do You favour those who deem
themselves to be wise in their own hearts.
Your loving kindness then is incomparable and
cannot be limited to our experience.
Your constant long is always for us to draw close
to You, to listen to Your heartbeat, to see as You
see and recognise the intricate knowledge of every
detail of our lives.
Every day You scan the whole earth seeking out
those whose heart is for You that You might walk
with them and strengthen them by Your words.
Amen

WATERS OF THE WORD

Deuteronomy 32:1-3

God, You revealed the essence of Your holiness
and wisdom through Your words to the prophets
of old. They were so sensitive to Your voice and
Your heart that You entrusted them with the deep
mysteries of Your desires and the blueprints of
how to walk in Your ways.
They shared Your commandments with the
people, speaking pure words from a heart that
honoured
Your holy name.
It was this sound, born of a heart of honour, that
caused the people to gather to listen and the
citizens of Heaven to take heed to every word that
was spoken. Even the earth thirstily drank up
every word they spoke, knowing it came directly
from Your mouth.
Even today Your word still falls like refreshing
rain into the hearts of those open to receive its
teaching, bringing restoration and a fullness of
life that can only be found in You
I will praise You My God of truth
Amen.

CRY OF A CHILD

Matthew 18:3

God, Your words to me as Your child constantly amaze me, for through them You show me how You are working behind the scenes to reveal Your wonders in my life.

How You long for us to speak with You; and ask for a greater understanding of these words of life that we might embrace them and take them deeper into our hearts.

Lord, give us a fresh desire to draw close to You in prayer and converse with You through travailing and prevailing prayers that see Your desires become evident in our lives.

Teach us more of Your ways, guiding us to walk with You in the paths that You have prepared for our lives, that the light of Your glory might shine brightly amid this dark world.

Amen.

FINDING THE FATHER'S HEART

Jeremiah 29:11, John 10:10, James 1:17

Lord, the mighty power of Your love is invincible;
nothing can stand against it or thwart the
purposes and plans You have decreed for our
lives.
In You we find a reason to live, to hope, for the
power of Your love will always be victorious, no
matter what we face, our future in You is secure.
Trusting in Your love is the only way by which we
can fully encounter Your truth and start to walk
on Your paths of life.
Father, it is only through Your grace, and the
favour You showed us through Jesus Your Son,
that we can come before You and receive Your
blessings, for outside of Your love we are and have
nothing.
I will praise Your name in daily gratitude for who
You are as my Father, for You embody all that is
good and right.
I put my life into Your hands.
Amen.

 THE GAZE OF THE KING

Psalm 139:23-24, Jeremiah 17:10

Lord, I invite You to come and search my heart
that You might expose the things which are not of
You that remain deeply hidden within me.
Your heart is for me to know the extreme depths
of Your love towards me, and for me to give You
permission to remove anything and everything
that is hindering my walk with You.
Lord, every word You speak to me is pure, being
both holy and righteous, for You are clothed in
majesty and Your authority comes from being
King of kings and Lord of lords.
Therefore, as the sovereign ruler of both heaven
and earth, let Your will be done through my life
today.
Amen.

KINGDOM TREASURES

Ephesians 1:3

Father God, I will praise You, for You have
empowered me with the authority of Your Son,
Jesus, and given me, by the Holy Spirit, every rich
gift made available within the Heavenly realm.
Thank You for equipping me with the powerful
truths in Your word, that through them I might
learn what it means to live a life of love and have
compassion for others.
Lord, when I read of Your promises to me and
Your divine instructions on how to deal with
those around me, I find I am drawn even closer to
You.
It is only by Your words that I find the strength to
put aside my selfish, sinful ways and simply trust
in You as my God.
Lead me deeper into the ancient paths of Your
word as You continue to make me righteous and
teach me how to live to the glory and honour of
Your name.
I know Your presence is always with me.
Amen.

CONSUMING FIRE

Hebrews 12:29

Lord God, the radiance of Your Heavenly glory
touches the earth in tendrils of fiery light.
Just as the sun radiates the light of its glory daily
upon the earth but is a ball of fire out in space, so
You are located in the Heavens and yet we feel the
warmth of Your power, the penetration of Your
goodness into every detail of our lives.
Every tree and flower find their strength in
drinking in the light of the sun. We too receive
Your life and power into our bodies by drinking
from the rich well of Your word and the presence
of Your glory.
You, O God, are the fire light that radiates in and
through our lives as we surrender wholly to You.
You are the consuming fire that burns
unrestricted in our hearts and whose glorious
authority shines through us as a beacon to others
living in this dark world.
Amen.

PERFECTED LOVE

1 John 4:18

Father, I am always amazed when I consider that
all things are under Your authority as God.
I know that nothing can stop Your words from
achieving their purpose and coming to pass
within my life. The Greatness of Your love is my
daily assurance, and the completion of Your
desires remains my constant focus.
Oh, how Your desire is for us to love You with the
same measure that You love us, to honour You
with the fullness of our thoughts longings and
desires that we might know You as intimately as
You know us.
Teach us not only to walk in the depths of Your
love but to also share that love with others
considering them as our brothers and sisters that
they also might come to know and walk with You.
Help us to leave our selfish ways behind and live
a life where You are our first priority as we seek
follow You in true love, humility
and in the fear of the Lord.
Amen

THE SOWER AND THE SEED

2 Corinthians 9:10

Lord, You are the only true giver of life.
When You surrendered Your Heavenly glory and
position to become a fleshly man, born of a virgin,
You also surrendered to become a seed of the
Father's word upon the earth.
As that seed You showed us the life and power
His words contained and invited us to live within
them daily. Likewise, as that seed You allowed
Your earthly covering to be broken as You died
and were hidden under the earth in a borrowed
tomb.
The full power of the life that was in You, as that
seed, was revealed as You resurrected and
brought forth the fullness of the Kingdom of God.
Seed is very precious to You for it was the image
You took on earth as the living word, and
therefore the enemy is intent on its destruction.
Come, Holy Spirit, and separate the good seed
of Your word, from the imitation seed of
deception in my life. Teach me to treasure and
protect the seed of Your word within me
Amen.

CHANGING HISTORY

Hebrews 13:8

Father, it is impossible for Your heart to change
towards me for Your love and Your presence in
my life followed me in my past, is present with me
now and will remain forever. I recognise it is still
Your desire to bring about change in my life.
Throughout history, through each season of life
You have always searched out a people, or a
person, whose heart longed after You. Your desire
was to use their lives to reveal the full strength of
Your authority and power, and so alter the course
of life of those around them.
I want to thank You, God, for everyone whose life
has been used to show me Your glory and to
extend Your Kingdom on the earth.
Thank You for everyone who surrendered their
own voice to become Your voice in my life and
whose ways taught me how to live out Your ways.
Lord, use me like You used them that I too might
be part of that purpose and contribute to the
change You are bringing on the earth.
Amen.

PERFECT PEACE

Matthew 11:28-29

God, I will place my trust in Your mighty strength,
as my Heavenly Father, for I know it is only in
You that I can find true rest and peace.
When I am weary and burdened by the weight of
all the expectations this world puts on me, I hear
You calling me to come into Your presence and
find true rest.
The world offers me many transitory things to
find respite, but they can never give me the
treasure of peace that I seek. It is beyond their
understanding both in how to attain it or how to
define it for it is only found in knowing I have
Your favour and that You delight in me.
Thank You for inviting me daily into Your secret
place, a place of quietness where Your presence is
found and where I can be alone with You, Jesus.
Amen.

ENCOUNTERING THE GAZE OF GOD

Job 32:8-9, Job 38:36

Lord God, Your authority is higher than every other authority, yet it is not Your words alone that define You as God, rather the life that You breath into them and release through them onto the earth.
It is Your life, as God, freely given to all who seek You that causes us to adore and worship You day by day and hour by hour,
It is the life within Your words that crowns each of our thoughts with wisdom and opens our hearts to Your presence that we might further understand and love You as our God.
It is the life within Your words, Your very breath as the Holy Spirit, that moves powerfully within our lives and draws us closer to You.
Many men have become great over the course of them, but few of them have sought You to receive Your wisdom. Even fewer have followed You to the end of their years in pursuit of comprehending the depths of Your justice and the everlasting nature of Your love
Amen.

DECLARATIONS OF GREATNESS

Job 38

Father, as I ponder the greatness of your glory, I find myself led deeper into Your peace. Every chapter of Your word I read gives me a greater revelation of who You are and reveals the strength of Your power in and over my life.

When I meditate on how You revealed Yourself throughout creation, I recognise how You set a boundary that neither fear nor destruction could not cross. You restored alignment and order by Your words and made the ways of the enemy to cease.

You set Yourself as a covering and in the likeness of cloud brought balance, structure and form into our chaos and confusion by speaking with words like thunder and proving Your arm to be strong.

Lord, may we take the time to stand still and consider all the wondrous works You've done for us and around us by the power of Your hand. May our knowledge of You be perfected by seeing with new eyes the wonders You display in the heavens and reveal upon the earth.

Amen.

THE QUEST FOR TRUTH

Ephesians 2:4-10

Father, the richness of mercy and love is
unequalled in value and the unlimited nature of
Your patience is beyond all comprehension.
Every day You move unseen in the invisible realm
that Your presence might surround us in all our
daily situations.
Lord, You speak Your thoughts and communicate
Your ways through many channels, that we might
learn to seek You further and see You in all things.
With every word You speak to us, You help us to
grasp the truth of Your living reality and drive us
to search out Your will and purpose
for our lives.
Open our ears and our eyes anew that we might
recognise both what Your Kingdom looks like on
earth and that we may walk with You as our God,
un-reliant on the ways of man.
Amen.

VESSELS OF HONOUR

Ephesians 3:10, Ephesians 3:16-19

Lord God, as ruler of the heavens and the earth,
You have granted us as Your church the wisdom
to discern the principalities and powers that
would seek to come against us and oppose Your
rule.
Father, may we, whom You have chosen as Your
own, be the living vessels through which You
show Yourself strong.
As the bearers and carriers of Your anointing,
may we bring healing to all those that call upon
Your name as we live lives that are strengthened,
rooted and grounded in Your love.
Let us shine as beacons of hope in our
communities revealing to those around us the
fullness of who You are, to the glory of Your
name.
Amen.

THE SON'S SACRIFICE

John 3:16, Ephesians 3:15, Ephesians 6:9

Father You love all the people You have created,
each individual matters dearly to You.
It was Your great love for us that led Your
Son, Jesus, to agree to surrender His Heavenly
position and status and to live among us as a man.
In doing so, He brought Your Kingdom onto the
earth and introduced You as our Father
through every detail of His life.
As both Your servant and as King, He showed us
what it meant to live lives of truth,
compassion, mercy, and forgiveness.
He was our sacrificial lamb,
who willingly laid down His life for us, choosing
to die on the cross, so we could receive the life
You longed to give us both now and for eternity.
Now we can come to You as both our God and
our Father for through Your Son, Jesus we
became Your children and were brought into
a family that inhabits both heaven and earth.
Amen.

UNDESERVED FAVOUR

Ephesians 5:2

Father, when I lie down beneath the stars, I
remember that You are the source.
Shadows might pass over them and cover the
earth, but even when I can no longer see the stars,
their light does not change. They are just one
example of a perfect gift You give me to remember
You.
Indeed, You overwhelm me with gifts each day
such is the greatness of Your love.
When I ponder on the depths of Your goodness, I
am amazed for I know I do not deserve Your
protection, provision, or an invitation into Your
peace, presence, and rest.
Yet it is Your desire to love me, and that desire
existed before I ever desired to love You in return.
Come, Holy Spirit, and saturate me with Your
love to the point of overflowing, that I might pour
it out in every relationship I share with people
and to those from every walk of life.
Amen.

CENTRE OF IT ALL

Genesis 2:7

God, it was Your great love and compassion that
led You to make man in Your own image and to
share with him Your breath and Your heart.
In doing so You became the centre of his life,
both spiritually and physically.
Lord, will You realign our hearts that we might
focus on You and seek Your presence in the
heavenly realms? For You are our true treasure
and our life is found solely in You.
Set our hearts on fire afresh that we might only
desire those things that are of You: Your words of
Truth and Your abundant lifegiving power as God.
Your greatest longing is for our hearts to once
more be established as Your own, that we might
love You fully with every part of our soul and
mind.
Amen.

KINGDOM ADVANCING

2 Corinthians 12:8-10

I will magnify and praise You, my God, I will
speak of Your majesty as the King enthroned in
Heaven and Your watchfulness over all the
kingdoms of the earth.
It delights You to make my weaknesses the source
of Your strength, as a testimony to others of the
power of Your great love and mercy.
As such my life becomes evidence of Your victory
and a banner of hope to those who seek to place
their trust in You.
Thank You for every time that You used my life
to be a source of preparation for someone else's
restoration.
I will daily speak of Your authority and move by
the leading of Your Holy Spirit that Your power
might be revealed through me.
Draw me closer and increase my hunger that I
might press fully into You and put into practice
the word of Your mouth.
Amen.

THE COLOURS OF CREATION

Romans 1:20

God, the splendour and glory of the Heavens and the breath-taking beauty of the earth leaves us in awe of You.

When we think about how Your spoken words brought everything into being, moving over them and heightening every detail to fine precision we are amazed.

Every creature is marked to according to Your specifications, the colours of every tree and flower were hand chosen by You.

How blessed we are to live surrounded by the green hues of nature, to gaze upon Your artistry in the sky and to listen to the tiny birds as they sing out their songs of joy and praise.

Continuously open our eyes, Lord that we might see daily fresh wonders of Your works and ways.

Amen.

BEHIND THE SCENES

Psalm 10:17

Lord God, not only do You listen
to every humble heartfelt prayer, but it is Your
perfect desire to answer it.
You both open our hearts to a greater
understanding of how You work unseen in our
daily lives and give us fresh revelation of Your
divine purposes for our future.
Lord, open our hearts and eyes afresh that we
might see all people as You see them through the
lenses of Your love
Then our hearts will never be troubled
by their words, nor we will live afraid of man,
but we will walk with You in wholehearted trust.
Amen.

COVERED BY HIS LOVE

Romans 7:15-20, Song of Songs 2:4

Lord, You are not blind to the condition of my heart: it is continuously exposed to Your sight and known intimately in all its ways.
In Your greatness You reveal its condition to me by Your words of authority even as You offer to cover and cocoon it with Your love.
Lord, You know that in my spirit I desire to do what is good, but in my own strength I lack the ability to carry it out. I long to obey what Your word invites me into but find it so hard to discipline myself to practice it daily.
I hate the fact that I am prone to yielding to my human nature instead of reflecting and living out Yours.
Lord, You alone can deliver me therefore I ask You, Holy Spirit, to come in Your glory and take the reign of my life that I might be fully Yours and live by the might of Your powerful name.
Amen.

THE WISDOM OF WARFARE

1 Chronicles 29:11, Psalm 2:4, Proverbs 2:6,
Isaiah 55:8

Lord God, I have no doubt that You are moving
powerfully behind the scenes. In the likeness of a
warrior, You have trained my arms for battle that
Your Kingdom might be established upon the
earth.
Nothing can stand against You for You already
have victory over all things. It is Your authority
and power that holds sway and rules over the
rulers of the nations.
You mockingly laugh at those who believe they
can tear down Your throne or cast off Your
wisdom for You are God.
What man can stand in opposition to You?
Everything a man thinks or does is but a vain and
fleeting puff of vapour compared to the power and
strength of Your thoughts and ways. How then
can they compare to You?
It is Your desires alone that can stand for having
declared in the heavens they are made manifest
on the earth.
Amen.

THE KING OF GLORY

1 Chronicles 29:11

Great is the power of Your victory, O Lord.
Glorious is the splendour of Your majestic rule
over the Heavens and the earth.
As Sovereign over Your Kingdom, O Lord, Your
authority is to be revered and respected over all.
I will praise Your name and surrender to Your
written words of wisdom, for my desire is to know
and embrace the mystery of who You are.
Yes, I will ponder Your glory when I look to the
heavens and exalt You as I gaze on Your
handiwork in the earth.
With every breath I will join with all Your
creation in adoring You as my Lord.
You alone are worthy of all my words and songs of
gratitude and joy, for unlike peoples' love, Your
love for us never grows cold.
Amen

THE LION AND THE LAMB

Psalm 68:8-9, 13, 33-35

Lord God, You ride in power upon the clouds
and give Your strength to those who look to You.
What is more precious than abiding in Your holy
place and hearing the authority in Your words as
You declare the excellence of Your riches to be
given to Your people?
How thankful we are, that as Gentiles, we have
been brought into Your family and declared by
Your authority to be Your own.
As our Shepherd Your power moves earth and
heaven on our behalf that we might enter Your
rest and be refreshed by Your life and care.
As the Lion You roar over our lives, shaking the
foundations and ensuring every hindrance and
obstacle is moved.
We will praise You, Lord.
Amen.

THE BLESSINGS OF OBEDIENCE

Proverbs 16:9

Lord God, whilst we might try to plan our own
ways in life, ultimately it is You who determine
our steps.
As we learn to trust in You and listen to the voice
of the Holy Spirit, You plant Your desires within
our hearts.
As we hear Your word and walk in obedience, we
find that we are richly blessed by You for it is
Your desire that we should receive every gift
available in the heavenly realms.
How mighty You are, O God. How awesome Your
love is that You would take the time and care to
single out every individual who needs a touch
from Your hand.
Lord, as we surrender to Your words and ways,
mould us into worthy vessels that we might carry
You into our world.
Amen.

LORD OF OUR LIVES

Psalm 8:4

Lord God, the vastness of the sea is Yours and the entire expanse of the earth belongs to You. Yet in the heavens, in the innermost room of Your dwelling place, You pace, consumed with thoughts
of us alone.
At the very beginning, Your thoughts were consumed by those You would create in Your image. Having created a world and made it ready for their arrival, You commanded the sun and moon to be their lights and the plants to yield them food.
Even now You show Your love and care for us for having sent Your Son as our Redeemer,
and given us eternal life, You also gave us the gift of the Holy Spirit that we might grow in our trust and live in the abundance of Your reality as God.
Amen.

ALMIGHTY ALIGNMENT

Genesis 50:2, Psalm 139, Isaiah 45:12,
1 Corinthians 14:33

Father, as the God of peace, You cannot tolerate
confusion or disorder.
It was You who intricately designed us, and it
delighted You to join our parts together and bring
forth Your wonder in our mothers' wombs.
It was by Your own hands that the beauty of the
heavens was stretched out that they might cover
us as a blanket.
You showed Your glory by creating us to reflect
and maintain the beauty of Your authority over
and above creation that all things might remain
aligned to Your words and will.
Since everything You do, O Lord, is precise
and for a purpose it is no wonder that You take
joy in turning everything that the enemy meant
for evil
into a testimony of Your goodness and to the glory
of Your name.
I will praise You, Lord.
Amen.

THE BELIEVERS' BREAD

John 6:33

Lord, Your word is powerful in its ability to pierce and change our hearts, yet it is also a gift of wonderous love freely given that we may learn more of You.
Every word written is both inspired by You and a feast of Your life. As we read and consume it, we find strength to believe that You Yourself dwell within us and will empower us to act it out.
Father, our desire is to become the light of Jesus in this dark, consumer focused, materialistic world.
Bind Your words into the very core of our hearts daily as You guide us and lead deeper in what it means to walk in Your eternal love through both forgiveness and obedience.
Amen.

<u>ABOVE ALL</u>

Isaiah 42:22, 25

Nothing can compare to the might of Your power,
my God, for You have no equal or rival from
anyone in the Heavens or on the earth.
Your glorious throne is established in the
Heavens and as the Lord and Commander of
Angel Armies, You are seated in majesty above
countless scores of angels who both adore You
and are obedient to Your bidding.
In the great magnitude of Your sovereignty, You
sit far above the tiny confines of the earth and we
who dwell on it are no more than grasshoppers.
How much more then is our worship and praise
due to You, O God? For all that You do and say is
marvellous and excellent beyond compare.
Teach us to meditate daily on Your greatness that
we might live out the fullness of Your word and
see the works of Your mighty hand
We, with the angels, will glorify Your name.
Amen.

CLOTHED IN COMPASSION

Psalm 86:15, Psalm 139, John 3:16, Romans 3:23

God, in Your boundless grace and compassion,
You have chosen to restrain Your anger against us
and instead favour us with abounding love and
faithfulness.
Your extreme love for us led You to forfeit Your
only Son as a ransom price to cover the vast debt
of sin. You allowed Him to take our place, to take
on the weight our sins and die on the Cross in
order that we might be truly set free.
How many times have we fallen short of Your
standards yet judged those around us for doing
the same? In Your eyes there is no distinction
between them and us.
Surely then our gratitude for the garments of
righteousness in which You clothe us, through our
trust in You as Lord, should far outweigh the need
to judge and speak out against others.
Come then, Lord, and examine our hearts anew.
Remove any offensive ways that remain within us
and silence our anxious thoughts.
Help us to always trust in You.
Amen.

FLEETING FOCUS

Psalm 39:5-6, Ephesians 5:16.

Lord God, when I think of how quickly the moments, seconds and hours pass by each day, I am struck by the reality that time is not my own to order it but moves beyond my control. How then can I align time back into Your purposes and plans for me? When I think of all the things I achieve in a day, I can count them on my hands. When I think of all I have spent my years on, it seems like nothing when I truly examine it from Your perspective. Even when I set myself with determined focus to do my best for You, I find the time flies by like a fleeting vapour, and what I'd hoped becomes a mere shadow in the light of embracing all You are. Yet I find solace in the truth that You have a special purpose for me to fulfil in life and that every moment, hour and day You are working that purpose out behind the scenes as I willingly surrender to Your desires and fix my focus on You. In Your hands each moment of time becomes a precious commodity and counts for something because You are moving within it and through it. Amen.

DESTINED TO GO DEEPER

Psalm 23, Psalm 138

Lord God, You constantly go before me in life,
preparing multiple ways for Your power and Your
glory to be revealed.
From the very beginning You established my path
and destiny to align to Your plans and ways of
advancing the Kingdom. By Your wisdom I am led
deeper into humility and find in that place that
my destiny in You is revealed.
In Your own life, the power of humility to advance
Your Kingdom is revealed.
From choosing a manger as Your unveiling to the
world, to the cross as the means of unveiling Your
reality as God, You showed that love, mercy,
forgiveness, and grace are birthed by great
sacrifice.
Lead me, Lord, in Your path of humility that I
also might become righteous and live solely for
Your name's sake.
Be magnified and adored by those who come to
see You through my obedience to Your Word and
my testimony of Your grace and favour.
Amen.

GOD'S GREATNESS REVEALED

2 Samuel 7:21-22, Isaiah 30:21, Revelation 22:13

Lord of Heaven, teach me the revelation of Your
greatness as 'I AM' for, from the beginning of time
unto its end, that is the identity You have chosen
by which to reveal Yourself.
As King from the very beginning, and the last and
eternal King who will reign, You have used the
splendour of Your mighty power to make Yourself
known throughout Your Word.
Teach me that I might know You and become
Your likeness, throwing down all false and
outward coverings that Your sovereignty might be
seen.
Open my eyes and understanding beyond all that
I have previously seen and heard of You, that I
might recognise You more as my Father and
discern Your hand in everything and everyone
You place around me.
Let me see and wonder at the intricate precision
of Your hand and purpose within Your creation
Open my ears to the powerful sound of Your voice
in all that I might discern Your ways anew and
walk within them
Amen.

THE EVERLASTING EYES OF LOVE

Psalm 139:1-5

God, in Your great love and mercy, You make it
Your quest to intimately know the heart of every
individual.
You stand beside them with eyes full of longing
and love. As they sit down at Your feet, You take
delight in sharing and knowing their thoughts and
laying Your hand upon them in blessing.
How worthy You are of our praise and adoration,
Lord, for You show us an amazing degree of
understanding and grace, pouring out
unconditional blessings upon those who love You.
Help us to live according to Your ways, Father,
and teach us to express the gratitude in our hearts
for every promise You have brought to pass by
Your mighty strength and Your powerful right
hand.
Amen.

FAITHFUL FRIEND

Psalm 23; Psalm 119: 89-91,173; Psalm 139:115,168

Every word You speak is recorded in Heaven and established eternally, enduring throughout the generations.
You spoke and the earth was established, abiding in Your presence, and living according to Your sovereign rule unto this very day.
Everyone who truly hears Your Word becomes Your servants, for it awakes in them the constant desire to be near to You, O Lord.
All Your commandments are the truth by which to live by and so I live daily before Your sight, dependant on Your mighty hand to help me obey them in such times as these.
Holy Spirit, I ask You to continually lead me and guide me by these words that I might become righteousness in Your sight.
I know that when I walk through times of trouble and despair, it is only Your Word that keeps my heart burning with life amid the shadows of death; for I am convinced that You are with me.
I will praise You, Mighty One.
Amen.

HIGH PRAISE

Psalm 139:5-6: Isaiah 25:1

I hold Your name in the highest regard, Lord.
I adore You for You have done wonderful things
in my life.
You have surrounded me like a protective hedge
and covered me in Your presence.
You have both defended me in times of trouble
and gone before me to prepare the path ahead
that I might have hope and enter the fullness of
Your goodness.
You have claimed me as Your own and in Your
desire for deeper relationship with me You given
me the gift of the Holy Spirit.
As my teacher and my comforter, Your Holy Spirit
has promised to guide me in the unseen paths of
Your realm, which are only revealed by
understanding the mystery of Your wisdom.
He has also promised to teach me Your desires
for my life that I might gain greater knowledge of
You; for it is too wonderful for me to grasp alone.
I want to express Your truth in the highest form of
praise as I place my trust in You, Lord.
Amen.

RELENTLESS LOVE

Psalm 23, Psalm 139:7, Revelation 4:11

O Lord, Your Holy Spirit constantly pursues me,
everywhere I go I feel His presence.
Even in my darkest hours He has been there,
telling me of Your nearness and Your loving
protection. They are evident and unmistakable.
As He relentlessly pursues me, He also guides me
into Your plans and purposes, revealing Your
faithfulness towards me as a Father and drawing
forth from me songs of praise.
When I think of Your provision, forgiveness,
patience and mercy towards me, I cannot help but
see how You have led me onto Your paths of
righteousness and arranged it so that others
might also know You.
You deserve and are worthy of all the glory and
honour I can ever give You, for You have endued
my life with Your power and made me Your own.
Amen.

WRITTEN BY THE WIND

Isaiah 55:8-9; Nahum 1:3

Lord, when I stand in the presence of a mighty
storm or feel the biting sting of strong winds
around me, I am reminded of Your great power.
Even the brooding clouds seem like the dust
caused by Your running feet as You race to bring
forth justice and judgement on my behalf.
Your thoughts towards me are far beyond my
comprehension for You cannot be identified by
my experiences and encounters with people.
Your means of judgement and justice are far
higher than that I've seen on the earth, therefore
in my times of trouble I will look to You and not
to people for help.
As my God and my wise Father, You are the only
one I can trust for I know the greatness of Your
love towards me will always result in all things
coming together for my good
Amen.

RIGHTEOUSNESS REVEALED

Psalm 46:1, Psalm 48:1, Acts 17:28

God, You are worthy to be praised, for You have
made Yourself our refuge from every evil on the
earth.
Even in the face of our enemies we find our
strength in Your greatness as King; for Your name
is magnified over all the earth and before You no-
one and nothing can stand.
All of creation is held captive to Your authority
and power, for its very life source and breath is
found in You as its Lord and Creator.
Therefore, as both the giver and sustainer of our
lives, we place our trust in You as the supreme
ruler of the nations, the one true God.
As we seek You in those times of trouble and
oppression, You are quick to encounter us and
inspire us with Your words, for You have
promised to remain near to each one of us and to
reveal Your glory as God on our behalf.
Amen.

THE WAY OF THE WORD

Psalm 23, Luke 11:24, John 6:68, 14:6, 1 John 3:1

Heavenly Father, Your Kingdom is established on
Your Word and Your glorious power.
This same Word and power created and
established everything within us and is the source
of our life day by day.
As Your children, passionately loved by You, we
look to You for guidance on how to walk in the
paths of life.
When we seek You in the mysteries of Your Word,
You encounter us in power and restore our souls.
The abundant life You give us through Your Word
is far beyond the transitory things that the world
has to offer, for every word holds the keys to
eternal life.
It is through Your words that we can come to You
as our Father and enjoy a deep and fulfilling
relationship with Jesus, Your Son.
Amen.

HUMILITY AND HONOUR

Psalm 119:160, Isaiah 42:8, Luke 11, John 3:16

God, the banner of Your glorious grace covers
every area of my life where You reign in victory.
As the great I AM, Your glory can never be taken
by another, for how they could match Your ways
or Your words for they are pure and full of truth?
Your voice is a clear sound to those who have ears
to hear You. To such, You show the greatness of
Your love and present them with their need for
the sacrifice of Your beloved Son, Jesus,
By His humility on the cross at Calvary the
greatest victory and honour, throughout the ages,
was won.
Now we declare Your greatness as God and bow
down before You, testifying to Your might as the
King above all kings.
Amen.

RIGHTEOUSNESS REVEALED

Philippians 4:6

God, Your righteousness is equal to Your glory.
Your word of truth thunders from the Heavens
bringing judgement and justice upon the earth.
When You speak words of peace into our hearts,
life's storms are stilled, and circumstances fade
away into nothing.
Your mercy drives You to enter our times of
trouble, to offer us hope by holding out Your hand
in an open invitation to walk with You.
Daily You lead and guide us through the difficult
situations that arrive, staying ever near to our
sides with the promise to remain.
What greater help or source of strength could we
have in times of trouble? Your goodness never
ends.
Your words are the beginning of our
breakthroughs, bringing life and light that
overcomes the shadows of depression and
despair.
Lord, let that light shine through my life daily.
Amen.

MEASURE OF HIS MAJESTY

Isaiah 40:12-13

Lord I am full of wonder when I behold Your
beauty and power as my King.
What man could give You counsel or dare to
direct Your hand? Your throne is established in
the heavens and Your feet hold the earth in
submission.
As the author of life, it is only by Your words that
everything finds its identity and purpose; even
our lives were written and planned out before we
were even born.
Lord, teach me the desires of Your heart and
bring me into Your purpose. Melt away any trace
of selfishness or pride and mould me as Your
servant into a pure vessel of honour, fit only for
Your use.
Let every word I speak bring forth life,
encouragement and healing to those around me.
Soften my heart and fill me afresh with Your
Spirit of righteousness.
Amen.

PURE LOVE

Matthew 6:9-13

Father, Your powerful words are so pure and
beautiful. The angels adore listening to them and
basking in the hidden revelations You bring forth
and reveal.
How we long to hear as they hear and to see You
as they see You, as one crowned in glorious light.
By Your words You invite us and draw us closer
that we too might behold and encounter these
truths and the life You've placed within them.
By the breath of Your Holy Spirit, You have made
us holy and by Your power we are invited to walk
with You and bring glory to Your name.
Father, forgive us when we have rejected this
invitation or taken our eyes away from You to
gaze on something else; when we have ignored
Your desires and battled against Your perfect
ways.
It is You and You alone who gives us the strength
to live through each day and therefore it is to You
that all our praise and adoration should be given.
Lord, make our lips pure fountains of praise both
today and for eternity.
Amen.

NAME ABOVE ALL NAMES

Philippians 2:9

Lord, I am in awe of You. From the Heavens Your
royal robes trail down, inscribed with words of
truth and righteousness.
Your authority is higher than any other.
Your name is above every other name. Every
spiritual being and principality knows its power
and must bow the knee before You.
Every word You speak is full of light bringing
healing, restoration, and wholeness to all who will
receive them and surrender to Your will.
I will praise Your Holy Name yes; I will praise You
my God for You are the source of all salvation.
Amen.

WORDS OF WONDER

Exodus 14, Luke 1:37, 24:2, Acts 12:3-19, 16:25-26

Lord, the strength of Your power is so vast that nothing is impossible for You to accomplish or bring forth on behalf of Your people.
By Your hand, the stone was rolled away that Your resurrected son might walk forth and usher in a new season of the Spirit.
By Your hand, chains were broken off Your people and prison doors swung open that Your word might be continually preached across the earth.
By Your hand, the seas were rolled back, the sun stopped, and the stars and clouds moved to guide Your people deeper on their journey of worship as they prepared to meet with You face to face.
Today You are still accomplishing wonders on behalf of Your people; weakness becomes strength and moral pride is humbled by the power of Your words.
Nothing You have set out to do, nothing You have spoken over us can ever be made void, for You actively involve Yourself in every detail of our lives that Your authority and power might be made known.
Amen.

TREES OF LIFE

Genesis 1:11, Luke 6:44, Song of Songs 2:3

Father, by Your wisdom, power, and authority
You brought all life into being.
As the Tree of Life, You became the source of the
air in the lungs of every living being. Even today,
every tree that stands benefits the life on earth by
providing oxygen and absorbing pollutants
through their leaves.
As with the fruit tree in the forest, You provided a
covering, strength and sweet fruit to eat and even
today every fruit tree offers shade, wood and fruit
for food.
You give them roots for strength, beauty in
appearance, seeds which hold seeds in
themselves. Every tree is known for its fruit and
every tree reflects Your nature and bountiful
provision.
Lord, never let us take these living reminders for
granted, forgive us and help us to gain a greater
revelation of how everything is sourced and
provided by Your hand.
Amen.

THE HEIGHTS OF HOLINESS

Psalm 139

Lord, if we were to measure the vast expanse of Your holiness, the whole world would not be able to hold it.

If we were to seek the fullness of Your vision and understanding, it would still be beyond our grasp though we sought for it all our lives. If we were to quest for the meaning of prayer, then we would become lost in the power of righteousness and tremble at the thunder in Your voice.

Oh, how You long for us to respond to Your heart and to hear with new ears the high reality of praise that is only known through Heavenly worship and heartfelt adoration.

What man can presume to know You, Father? To claim to comprehend and understand God? Yet You knew each of us before we were born, having knitted and joined us together in secret. We are still searching to know You, yet You are familiar with every tiniest detail of our daily lives.

Nothing is hidden from You. Nothing is excluded from Your vision, for You know all, are present in all and work in all things to reveal to us Your love.

Amen.

INFINITE POWER

Psalm 103:14, Jeremiah 18, Colossians 3:3

The infinite power of Your love and mercy
towards us, Lord, is everlasting in its endurance,
for our lives are bound up in Yours.
Our hearts do not have the capacity to hold the
magnitude of the revelation of who You are,
therefore give us a greater understanding that we
might know what You desire and how to walk in
Your ways.
Show us the extent of Your authority as the God of
Heaven, the Son who rules the earth and the Holy
Spirit who rules and moves within the spiritual
realm, that we might turn in repentance from the
pride of our own thinking and limited
understanding. Yours are the hands that made us.
Without Your life breathing and moving in us we
are nothing but dust.
Come then, Holy Spirit, and mould us as living
clay into vessels that bring honour and glory to
Your name. Empty us of ourselves and fill us
afresh with Your power that we might be filled to
overflowing and that Your authority might be
made known.
Amen

TEMPLES OF HIS GLORY

Acts 7:48, 17:24, 1 Corinthians 6:19-20

Father God, when You ripped the veil of the
temple, and departed from it at the death of Your
son, You announced the end of Your dwelling in
man-made temples and heralded in the beginning
of Your dwelling in man.
By the blood of Jesus, every person from every
nation was invited to joined as one in You through
the power, life, and breath of the Holy Spirit; that
through their lives You might dwell and move in
every place upon the earth.
How then can we be distant and separated from
You when You dwell within us and give us the
strength to live and to move?
Are not our bodies now the temple of the Holy
Spirit who was given to us at Your Son's request
and who now resides with us daily?
How then can we be owners of our lives when
those same lives were brought back by You at a
great cost at the cross of Calvary?
No, we are Yours. Your glory covers us and dwells
in us by Your Spirit and by His life in us we have
been made and are being made holy.
Help us, O Lord, to surrender to Your Spirit's
leading to the praise of Your Holy name. Amen.

LIGHTS IN THE DARKNESS

Matthew 5:16, John 1:9, Psalm 119:105

Lord God, the light of Your glory is so great that the shadows of darkness cannot remain in Your presence. As You walk before me and beside me, my daily path becomes illuminated, and every trace of shadow is forced to flee.
Your glory is so pure, so holy and so blinding that even to encounter Your presence is to encounter a consuming fire, so bright that men's eyes are blinded simply by looking upon You.
Oh, what a mystery it is when You declare that same glorious light to be seen on us and in us by those we encounter daily, becoming impossible for them not to witness Your goodness and Your power as God.
How great and how bright that light shines when we daily pursue You and walk with You in intimate relationship, when we seek to know You more. It is only in the secret place of prayer that You unveil our eyes that we might see You clearly.
Oh, how much more, having caught a glimpse of You will we seek to love You and to pursue You daily.
Amen.

RIVERS OF BLESSING

Psalm 19:14, Jeremiah 17:10

Father, every blessing we have received is given to
us from Your hand, by the Spirit of life, to cleanse
our hearts and give us divine inspiration
concerning Your will and Your ways.
How different are our own thoughts to Yours?
How different our words and the meditations of
our hearts?
Lord make them acceptable in Your sight again by
transforming our words into Your words of life
and bringing the light of Your glory into ever
thought and motive. Guide us deeper into
relationship with You that every action might
speak of the presence of Your life within us.
Call us and draw us nearer and nearer to You by
capturing our ears with the sweet sound of Your
voice. By Your words teach us and strengthen our
obedience as we apply them to our lives.
Lord, nurture our trust in You as we gaze afresh
on the life, words, and character of Your Son for
in truly seeing Him we will also see You and
become Your reflection on the earth.
Amen.

WORDS OF TRANSFORMATION

Psalm 91:11, 104:19

The awesomeness of Your power, O God, fills the Heavens. From Your all-seeing eyes, not one detail of life on earth is hidden.
If You but uttered the word, the course of the earth, moon, stars, and sun would change, transforming our lives forever. It is only by Your grace and mercy that our lives are protected for every day You choose to walk beside us in Your power. You have appointed warrior angels to watch over us and keep us under the safety and authority of Your Word.
Each word brings light into the shadows, destroying the powers of sin and pride and releasing the promise that by Your Spirit we could live free from judgement and condemnation.
Over and over Your prophetic words and signs have changed the course of mankind and invited them to pursue You, yet in our selfishness we often choose to continue walking in our own ways.
Thank You, Lord, that Your words are still being given to us through Your Son that we might live in increasing relationship with You.
Amen.

FAITHFUL TO FIGHT FOR US

Psalm 46:1, 138:2, Hebrews 6:18, Deuteronomy 31:6, Isaiah 41:10

God, in times of trouble and trial, I will look to You as my source, for by Your mighty strength every fear is vanquished, and every foe defeated. Great is Your courage, everlasting is Your might, in that You continue to fight on our behalf having called and predestined us to live within these days?

Empower our hearts with faith that we might stand firm knowing You are with us, that the strength of the Holy Spirit dwells within us and that Your hand is holding us steady in every circumstance.

Your faithfulness is indisputable. You are entirely trustworthy for You are always aware of what is happening to us and will never leave us to face it alone.

When You speak, You speak the truth and act upon it, therefore, make our hearts as faithful to trust in You as You are to uphold and bring to pass what You have promised.

Your greatness, Your nearness, Your might and Your truth are real and unprecedented, therefore we choose to put our trust in You.

Amen.

UNFATHOMABLE MYSTERIES

Psalm 139:6, Ecclesiastes 1:7

God, Your wisdom is unfathomable; Your ways
mysterious; Your love immeasurable and Your
power unshakable.
Every form of life within the oceans and the seas
praises You for they recognise You as their
Creator and Sustainer.
Every tree, flower, plant and fruit come forth in
beauty and life to bless You as their Creator and
to be a reminder of You to man.
Night by night, day by day, the artistry of the skies
speaks of Your glory and the Mazzaroth of the
stars tell out the great stories of the past, the
promises for today and the eternal salvation and
victory which is to come.
I will praise You O God.
Amen.

PREVAILING PRESENCE

Psalm 139:7-12, John 14:12

Lord, Your presence is everywhere. No-one in their heart of hearts can deny it or stand against the reality that You are both God and the source of life.
You see all and know all for You are present in every sphere of influence, every place of authority, every home and dwelling, from the rich to the extremes of poverty.
Yours is the power alone to drive out demons, to bring the dead to life and to make healing manifest through the lives, hands, and words of those who seek Your heart and Your will.
Lord, I look daily for evidence of Your works and wonders in the lives of those around me and in connection to me, but I see little evidence of those miracles that were recorded and testified in Your word.
O Lord, You are the true discerner of men's hearts. Capture my heart fully that I might pursue You and, in my surrender, bring about the manifestation of Your wonders and testify to the truth in Your words.
Amen.

AUTHOR OF THE NEW

John 7:37-38, Isaiah 43:18-19

Lord, all Your ways are awesome, Your words of
wisdom powerful, and the mystery of how You
made all things in Heaven and Earth
unfathomable to men's minds.
By the power of Your Spirit, You made the
surrounding waters of the earth part that You
might bring forth life. In the same way that we are
surrounded by waters at birth and at baptism, we
are also released by the Spirit at Your Word and
invited to enter a new life.
Having been made new, we must forget what has
happened in the past and all the words and
traditions we have built our lives upon, that we
might gaze and recognise the new things You are
doing in our lives.
By the power of Your Spirit, Your promises are
springing forth to life within us, bringing life and
a satisfaction in Your presence that the world
cannot compete with. As we drink daily of Your
words, our hearts become flooded by Your Spirit
and pour forth as life to all those around us.
Lord, may I always long to drink of Your words of
life that I might become a fountain of praise that
brings honour to Your name.
Amen.

Printed in Great Britain
by Amazon

74267900R00088